Language Activity Book
Student's Edition

ECCE ROMANI

A Latin Reading Program
Second Edition

I-B
Rome at Last

Longman

Longman, 10 Bank Street, White Plains, NY 10606

Associated companies:
Longman Group Ltd., London
Longman Cheshire Pty., Melbourne
Longman Paul Pty., Auckland
Copp Clark Pitman, Toronto

ISBN: 0-8013-1210-8 Student's Edition
ISBN: 0-8013-1214-0 Teacher's Edition

23 24 25 26 27   11 10 09

CHAPTER 18 | ARRIVAL AT THE INN

Activity 18a
Fill in the blanks with Latin words to match the English cues:

1. Cornēlius puerōs quī _____ identidem revocāvit. (were running ahead)

2. Cornēliī ad caupōnam appropinquābant et subitō canēs ad eōs

   _____ _____ . (hurl themselves)

3. _____ _____

   _____ et canēs revocāvit. (A fat man appeared)

4. "_____ canēs caudās movent _____ , quod laetī sunt." (These) (only)

5. "_____ _____ !" ("Don't flee!"; pl.)

6. Puella sōla ad canēs manum _____ . (holds out)

7. "Multī _____ praeclārī hīc pernoctāvērunt," inquit Apollodōrus. (guests)

8. "_____ hīc in caupōnā _____ prīncipis pernoctāvit." (Once) (an envoy)

9. Aurēlia mussat, "_____ quod in caupōnā pernoctāre necesse est." (I am sad)

10. "_____ _____ , caupō est meus amīcus Apollodōrus!" inquit Eucleidēs. (Unless I am mistaken)

11. "_____ _____ , mī Apollodōre?" (How are you?)

Activity 18b

cauda, -ae, f.
lēgātus, -ī, m.
plaustrum, ī, n.
homō, hominis, m.
ars, artis, f.
onus, oneris, n.

Supply the proper form of *omnis, -is, -e* before each of the following nouns and the proper form of *noster, nostra, nostrum* after each noun. Be sure to make the adjectives agree with the nouns in gender, case, and number. The words used are in the box at the left:

omnis, -is, -e		*noster, nostra, nostrum*
1. _____	caudam	_____
2. _____	artēs (nom. pl.)	_____
3. _____	lēgātō	_____
4. _____	plaustrum	_____
5. _____	onere	_____
6. _____	lēgātus	_____
7. _____	ars	_____

8. _____ caudae (gen. sing.) _____

9. _____ hominem _____

10. _____ caudīs _____

11. _____ lēgātōrum _____

12. _____ artem _____

13. _____ hominibus _____

14. _____ plaustra _____

15. _____ cauda _____

16. _____ onerum _____

17. _____ caudae (nom. pl.) _____

18. _____ oneris _____

19. _____ hominum _____

20. _____ plaustrī _____

21. _____ arte _____

22. _____ caudārum _____

23. _____ onera _____

24. _____ artibus _____

25. _____ homine _____

Activity 18c

In the following sentences, the most important clues of meaning are those of agreement of adjectives. Sometimes words appear in an unusual order with adjectives separated from the nouns they modify. Translate each sentence:

1. Canis magnus ossa habet. _____

2. Canis magna ossa habet. _____

3. Ossa multī canēs habent. _____

4. Canis magnum os habet. _____

5. Omnia ossa magnus canis habet. _____

6. Magna habent multī canēs ossa. _____

7. Magnum canis habet os. _____

os, ossis, n., *bone*

Activity 18d
Translate into Latin:

1. Aurelia was going toward the inn slowly because she did not want to spend the night there.

   _____

2. Suddenly three dogs bark fiercely and attack the Cornelii.

   _____

3. Cornelia holds out her hand to the dogs and they wag their tails.

   _____

4. At that very moment a fat man appeared at the door of the inn and greeted the guests.

   _____

   _____

5. Eucleides happily shouts, "I recognize my friend Apollodorus!"

   _____

6. The innkeeper replies, "I am glad that you are coming to my inn. Come in, everyone!"

   _____

   _____

Activity 18e
Give the Latin word to which each of the following English words is related and give the meaning of the English word:

	Latin Word	*Meaning of the English Word*
1. coda	_____	_____
2. legate	_____	_____
3. obese	_____	_____
4. canine	_____	_____
5. precipitate	_____	(verb) _____
		(adjective) _____
6. hospitable	_____	_____
7. apparition	_____	_____
8. manual	_____	(adjective) _____
		(noun) _____
9. irrevocable	_____	_____
10. hospital	_____	_____

CHAPTER 19

SETTLING IN

Activity 19a

Write the missing forms of each verb in the proper columns. The first set is done for you:

Present 3rd Sing.	Perfect 3rd Sing.	Present 3rd Plur.	Perfect 3rd Plur.
intrat	_intrāvit_	_intrant_	intrāvērunt
_____	iussit	iubent	_____
dūcit	dūxit	_____	_____
_____	_____	gemunt	gemuērunt
videt	_____	_____	vīdērunt
_____	explicāvit	explicant	_____
advenit	advēnit	_____	_____

Activity 19b

Fill in the endings on the adjectives in the following passage:

Servī caupōnis obēs_____ diū labōrābant, sed raedam immōbil_____ ē

magn_____ fossā extrahere nōn poterant. Servī dēfess_____ ad caupōnam

vīcīn_____ redeunt. Brev_____ tempore caupō īrāt_____

omn_____ servōs convocāvit. "Necesse est mult_____ hōrās labōrāre," inquit

caupō. "Ego nōn senātōrem praeclār_____ sed uxōrem molest_____ timeō.

Crās vōcem magn_____ uxōris īrāt_____ audīre nōlō. Strēnuē igitur labōrāte!"

Activity 19c

Rewrite the following sentences changing all nouns, adjectives, and verbs from singular to plural:

1. Caupō obēsus equum ad raedam immōbilem dūxit.

   _____

2. Fīlia senātōris praeclārī in magnā urbe habitāvit.

   _____

3. Māter misera ancillae in agrō dominī etiam labōrāvit.

   _____

4. Tabellārius sēmisomnus per viam perīculōsam iter longum fēcit.

   _____

bonus
brevis
dēfessus
fortis
ignāvus
īnfirmus
īrātus
laetus
longus
magnus
meus
miser
multus
noster
omnis
scelestus
sollicitus
sordidus
temerārius
tuus

Activity 19d

Select an adjective from the box at the left to describe each of these nouns. Be sure to make the adjectives agree with the nouns in gender, case, and number. Try to use each adjective only once:

1. hospitem _____
2. lēgātus _____
3. caudās _____
4. hominēs (acc. pl.) _____
5. dominī (gen. sing.) _____
6. aedificia _____
7. vōcis _____
8. puellārum _____
9. iter _____
10. perīculō _____
11. equōs _____
12. lectīs _____
13. prīncipum _____
14. ancillae (gen. sing.) _____
15. frātribus _____
16. senātōre _____

Activity 19e

Fill in the blanks with Latin words to match the English cues:

1. "_____ mē ad cubiculum meum!" ("Take . . . !")
2. Aurēlia est _____ dēfessa. (very)
3. Servus cēnam _____ parāvit. (for Cornelius)
4. Multī _____ in caupōnā Apollodōrī pernoctāvērunt. (travelers)
5. Servī _____ _____ parant. (another bed)
6. "Hic lectus est _____," inquit Aurēlia. (better)
7. Servus _____ bonam Marcō et Sextō parāvit. (dinner)
8. Nūllī senātōrēs ad caupōnās _____ _____ . (are in the habit of coming)
9. Ubi Apollodōrus _____ _____ temptāvit, Aurēlia eum reprehendit. (to explain the situation)
10. "Nōn necesse est _____ mē reprehendere," inquit caupō. (for you)
11. Puerī _____ volunt quod _____ . (to dine) (they are hungry)
12. Cornēlia dēfessa _____ _____ vult. (to go to bed)

Activity 19f

Translate into Latin:

1. Cornelius was worried because all inns were dangerous and many innkeepers were wicked.

_____

_____

2. He entered the large inn, however, and ordered the fat innkeeper to prepare a good dinner.

_____

3. Cornelius was dining with all the travelers.

_____

4. Suddenly Aurelia groaned because the bedroom was dirty.

_____

5. Soon the slaves of the innkeeper carried a better bed into the bedroom.

_____

_____

6. Cornelius' tired wife was able to go to bed.

_____

Activity 19g

For each italicized English word below, give the Latin word to which the English word is related. Then complete each clause with the meaning of the English word. The first set is done for you:

Latin Word	*If you are—*	*Meaning of the English Word*
reprehendere	**1.** behaving in a *reprehensible* manner, your actions are	blameworthy
_____	**2.** protesting *vehemently*, you are doing so	_____
_____	**3.** revealing a *sordid* secret, you are telling something that is	_____
_____	**4.** listening to the *explication* of a difficult problem, you are hearing an	_____
_____	**5.** being carried in a *litter*, you are reclining on a	_____
_____	**6.** picking up *litter*, you are collecting	_____
_____	**7.** the owner of a *litter* of puppies, you have a	_____
_____	**8.** removing a *coverlet*, you are taking off the	_____
_____	**9.** *exploiting* your talents, you are	_____
_____	**10.** speaking *explicitly*, you are saying things very	_____

CHAPTER 20

CHANCE ENCOUNTER

Activity 20a

Fill in the corresponding forms for the missing tenses (the first is done for you):

Present	Imperfect	Perfect
1. mittis	*mittēbās*	*mīsistī*
2. _____	tenēbant	_____
3. _____	_____	audīvimus
4. petō	_____	_____
5. _____	habēbātis	_____
6. gemis	_____	_____
7. est	_____	_____
8. _____	iaciēbam	_____
9. _____	_____	intrāvimus
10. _____	iubēbant	_____

Activity 20b

Deduce and give the first three principal parts for each verb:

	1st Sing. Present	Present Infinitive	1st Sing. Perfect
1. rīdēs, rīsistī			
2. faciunt, fēcērunt			
3. cadimus, cecidimus			
4. stātis, stetistis			
5. venīs, vēnistī			
6. dīcunt, dīxērunt			
7. concidimus, concidimus			
8. fugiunt, fūgērunt			
9. ascendit, ascendit			
10. pōnitis, posuistis			
11. vidēs, vīdistī			
12. extrahit, extrāxit			
13. movent, mōvērunt			
14. trādunt, trādidērunt			
15. surgis, surrēxistī			
16. scrībis, scrīpsistī			

17. dēvertō, dēvertī   _____ _____ _____

18. excipiunt, excēpērunt   _____ _____ _____

19. adiuvās, adiūvistī   _____ _____ _____

20. sedet, sēdit   _____ _____ _____

21. cōnspiciō, cōnspexī   _____ _____ _____

22. legunt, lēgērunt   _____ _____ _____

23. gerit, gessit   _____ _____ _____

24. reprehendunt, reprehendērunt _____ _____ _____

25. quiēscunt, quiēvērunt   _____ _____ _____

26. cōnsulimus, cōnsuluimus _____ _____ _____

27. currit, cucurrit   _____ _____ _____

28. respondēs, respondistī _____ _____ _____

29. repellitis, reppulistis _____ _____ _____

30. arripiunt, arripuērunt _____ _____ _____

31. agimus, ēgimus   _____ _____ _____

Activity 20c
Fill in the blanks with Latin words to match the English cues:

1. Flāvia et Cornēlia cubitum īvērunt, sed Marcus et Sextus cum Cornēliō

   _____ . (stayed)

2. Ad mediam noctem _____ in animō habuērunt. (to stay awake)

3. Marcus et Sextus ēsuriunt et Marcus rogat, "_____

   _____ hīc cēnāre?" (May we)

4. _____ tacēbat pater. (For a short time)

5. Tandem, "_____ !" inquit. ("All right!")

6. Rīsērunt puerī quod laetī erant. Voluērunt _____ ibi cēnāre et aliōs viātōrēs spectāre. (for)

7. Dum puerī cibum _____ , subitō intrāvit

   _____ _____ . (devour) (a certain soldier)

8. "Salvē, _____ _____ ," inquit. (sir)

9. "Cūr vōs _____ _____

   _____ intrāvistis?" (into this inn)

10. "Quod raeda nostra in fossā _____

    _____ ," respondet Cornēlius. (is stuck fast)

(continued)

11. "In agrīs _____ manēre nōlēbāmus, sed _____

_____ in caupōnā pernoctāvimus."(at night) (never before)

12. Tum mīles, "In caupōnā," inquit, "pernoctāre saepe est _____."
(dangerous)

13. "Audīvī fābulam _____ caupōne quī hospitem

_____ ." (about) (killed)

14. "Volō _____ fābulam dē caupōne _____."
(that famous) (to tell)

15. "Nōbīs illam fābulam _____ , mīles!" inquit Cornēlius. (tell)

16. "_____ audīte!" inquit mīles. (Attentively)

Activity 20d
Translate into Latin:

1. The boys wanted to eat dinner and stay awake until midnight, but Cornelius ordered them to go to bed.

_____

_____

2. For inns are dangerous at night.

_____

3. Cornelius was afraid because he heard a story about an innkeeper who killed two guests.

_____

_____

4. The boys went to bed frightened.

_____

5. They stayed awake for a long time.

_____

Activity 20e
Give the Latin word to which each of the following English words is related and give the meaning of the English word:

	Latin Word	*Meaning of the English Word**
1. militate	_____	_____
2. vigilant	_____	_____
3. vigilante	_____	_____
		_____

* An English dictionary may be needed for this exercise.

	Latin Word	*Meaning of the English Word*

4. auditorium _____   _____

    _____

5. license _____   a. _____

    b. _____

    _____

    c. _____

6. illicit _____   _____

Activity 20f
Find the meanings of the following Latin expressions that occur in English:

1. ante-bellum _____

2. post-bellum _____

3. ante meridiem _____

4. post meridiem _____

5. post mortem _____

Activity 20g
To what Latin word are all of the following English words related? _____.
Look up each of the following words in an English dictionary and write a definition
of it that will show how the English word incorporates the meaning of the Latin
word to which all of these words are related:

1. dictate a. _____

    _____

    b. _____

    _____

2. dictionary _____

    _____

3. predict _____

    _____

4. edict _____

    _____

5. indict _____

    _____

CHAPTER 21 MURDER

Activity 21a

Fill in the missing principal parts and give the conjugation numbers or irreg. for irregular verb in the parentheses at the right:

1. _____ _____ posuī _____ ( )

2. _____ _____ _____ surrēctūrus ( )

3. _____ removēre _____ _____ ( )

4. inveniō _____ _____ _____ ( )

5. _____ _____ iussī _____ ( )

6. _____ _____ _____ adiūtus ( )

7. _____ īre _____ _____ ( )

8. dīcō _____ _____ _____ ( )

9. _____ _____ petīvī _____ ( )

10. _____ _____ _____ iactus ( )

11. _____ esse _____ _____ ( )

12. _____ _____ _____ vīsus ( )

13. _____ dūcere _____ _____ ( )

Activity 21b

Fill in the blanks with the correct form of the verb in parentheses in the perfect tense:

1. Cūr vōs nōndum _____ , puerī? (surgere)

2. Valdē doleō, domine, quod ego fossam nōn _____ . (vidēre)

3. Caupō servōs ad raedam statim _____ . (mittere)

4. Quō vōs equōs _____ , servī? (dūcere)

5. Servī caupōnis raedam ē fossā nōn _____ . (extrahere)

6. Quid tū _____ , Aurēlia? (dīcere)

7. Ego, mea domina, alium lectum tibi _____ . (invenīre)

8. Nōs laetī amīcōs _____ . (adiuvāre)

9. Quandō tū cubitum _____ ? (īre)

10. Illā nocte nōs omnēs dēfessī _____ . (esse)

11. Ego tē _____ fābulam nārrāre. (iubēre)

12. Caupō corpus Aulī in plaustrum _____ . (iacere)

13. Septimus ē plaustrō corpus amīcī _____ . (removēre)

14. Cīvēs statim caupōnem scelestum _____ . (petere)

15. "Cūr tū mē _____ , domine?" rogāvit caupō. (accūsāre)

Activity 21c

In each set below, one verb does not belong because in numbers 1–5 it is not the same tense as the others and in numbers 6–10 it is not the same person and/or number as the others.

Circle the verb that does not belong in each group:

1. portāvērunt	sunt	removēmus	dormīmus
2. poterās	erāmus	faciēbās	extrahimus
3. adiūvērunt	fuit	dīximus	invenītis
4. pūniēbat	poterat	est	clāmābat
5. habuistis	cōgitātis	pūnītis	timētis
6. poteram	eō	parāvistī	posuī
7. es	appāruī	iussistī	lacrimās
8. facimus	iēcimus	agitis	sedēmus
9. sum	necāvī	ībam	vīdistī
10. nōn vīs	appropinquāvistī	poterat	erās

Activity 21d

Fill in the blanks with Latin words to match the English cues:

1. "_____ _____ ," inquit caupō.
"Intrāte, viātōrēs!" (There is nothing wrong)

2. Aurēlia _____ caupōnam intrāvit. (unwilling)

3. Postquam cēnam _____ , mīles fābulam nārrāvit. (we finished)

4. "Meum _____ valdē timeō," _____
Septimus. (dream) (thought)

5. Aulus _____ _____ nōn poterat. (to regain his senses)

6. Caupō _____ _____ corpus iēcit.
(dung) (on top of)

7. Septimus ad caupōnam _____ _____
iter fēcit. (at dawn)

8. Caupō _____ scelestus _____ . (to him) (seems)

9. Septimus Aulum _____ sub stercore invēnit. (dead)

10. Puerī, _____ fābulam audīvērunt, valdē timēbant. (after)

11. Sextus, quamquam ad cubiculum iit, nōn _____ . (did . . . fall asleep)

12. Puerōs, quod _____ cubitum iērunt, pater
_____ . (late) (punished)

13. Canēs lātrantēs Marcum ē _____ māne excitāvērunt. (sleep)

14. Ubi corpus _____ vīdit, caupō
_____ simulāvit. (of Aulus) (innocence)

Activity 21e
Match each verb with its correct translation:

_____	1. iaciunt	a. they have thrown
		b. we kept throwing
_____	2. removet	c. we are sending
_____	3. mīsimus	d. they are throwing
_____	4. removēbant	e. I did remove
		f. he does remove
_____	5. iēcistī	g. we were sending
_____	6. remōvit	h. you do send
_____	7. mittitis	i. they were removing
		j. you were throwing
_____	8. removeō	k. we have sent
_____	9. iaciēbāmus	l. you kept sending
		m. you threw
_____	10. mittēbās	n. I remove
_____	11. iēcērunt	o. she removed
_____	12. mittimus	
_____	13. remōvī	
_____	14. mittēbāmus	
_____	15. iaciēbās	

Activity 21f
Translate into Latin:

1. Once Aulus was making a journey in Greece.

   _____

2. He could not find his friend's country house, and so he spent the night in an inn.

   _____

   _____

3. When the innkeeper saw the tired traveler, he ordered slaves to help him.

   _____

   _____

4. But that night he killed (his) poor guest.

   _____

5. In the morning he hid the body under the dung in a wagon.

   _____

6. When the citizens removed the dung and saw Aulus dead, they loudly accused the innkeeper and punished him.

   _____

   _____

Activity 21g

For each italicized English word below, give the Latin word(s) to which the English word is related. Give Latin verbs in infinitive form. Then complete each statement. The first is done for you:

Latin word(s)	*If you are—*	
petere	**1.** distributing a *petition*, you are . . . signatures.	seeking
_____ _____	**2.** a *somnambulist*, you are a	_____
_____	**3.** receiving *corporal* punishment, you are receiving punishment to your	_____
_____	**4.** *immortal*, you will not	_____
_____	**5.** *cogitating*, you are	_____
_____	**6.** a person of *infinite* wisdom, your wisdom has no	_____
_____	**7.** making a *deposit*, you are . . . something down	_____
_____	**8.** *corpulent*, you have a large	_____
_____	**9.** considering *punitive* measures, you are looking for ways to	_____
_____	**10.** a general's *adjutant*, you are the general's	_____
_____	**11.** in a *mortuary*, you are surrounded by	_____
_____	**12.** *simulating*, you are	_____

VOCABULARY FOR REVIEW

NOUNS

1st Declension

Asia, -ae, f., *Asia Minor*

cauda, -ae, f., *tail*

cēna, -ae, f., *dinner*

culīna, -ae, f., *kitchen*

fābula, -ae, f., *story*

Graecia, -ae, f., *Greece*

innocentia, -ae, f., *innocence*

Megara, -ae, f., *Megara (a city in Greece)*

pecūnia, -ae, f., *money*

pīrāta, -ae, m., *pirate*

2nd Declension

aurum, -ī, n., *gold*

crotalum, -ī, n., *castanet*

lectus, -ī, m., *bed, couch*

lēgātus, -ī, m., *envoy*

somnium, -ī, n., *dream*

somnus, -ī, m., *sleep*

3rd Declension

corpus, corporis, n., *body*

fēlēs, fēlis, gen. pl., fēlium, f., *cat*

Gādēs, Gādium, f. pl., *Gades (Cadiz, a town in Spain)*

homō, hominis, m., *man*

lībertās, lībertātis, f., *freedom*

lūx, lūcis, f., *light*

mīles, mīlitis, m., *soldier*

mors, mortis, gen. pl., mortium, f., *death*

mūs, mūris, m., *mouse*

saltātrīx, saltātrīcis, f., *dancer*

stercus, stercoris, n., *dung, manure*

viātor, viātōris, m. *traveler*

ADJECTIVES

1st and 2nd Declension

invītus, -a, -um, *unwilling*

malus, -a, -um, *bad*

medius, -a, -um, *mid-, middle of*

nārrātus, -a, -um, *told*

obēsus, -a, -um, *fat*

optimus, -a, -um, *best, very good*

prīmus, -a, -um, *first*

sordidus, -a, -um, *dirty*

timidus, -a, -um, *afraid*

tōtus, -a, -um, *all, the whole*

3rd Declension

fortis, -is, -e, *brave, strong*

omnis, -is, -e, *all, the whole, every, each*

VERBS

1st Conjugation

accūsō, -āre, -āvī, -ātus, *to accuse*

adiuvō, adiuvāre, adiūvī, adiūtus, *to help*

agnōscō, agnōscere, agnōvī, agnitus, *to recognize*

appellō, -āre, -āvī, -ātus, *to call, name*

cantō, -āre, -āvī, -ātus, *to sing*

cēnō, -āre, -āvī, -ātus, *to dine, eat dinner*

cōgitō, -āre, -āvī, -ātus, *to think*

dēvorō, -āre, -āvī, -ātus, *to devour*

dō, dare, dedī, datus, *to give*

errō, -āre, -āvī, -ātūrus, *to wander, be mistaken*

explicō, -āre, -āvī, -ātus, *to explain*

laudō, -āre, -āvī, -ātus, *to praise*

lavō, lavāre, lāvī, lautus, *to wash*

nārrō, -āre, -āvī, -ātus, *to tell (a story)*

necō, -āre, -āvī, -ātus, *to kill*

parō, -āre, -āvī, -ātus, *to prepare, get ready*

praecipitō, -āre, -āvī, -ātus, *to hurl*

recuperō, -āre, -āvī, -ātus, *to recover*

saltō, -āre, -āvī, -ātūrus, *to dance*

simulō, -āre, -āvī, -ātus, *to pretend*

vigilō, -āre, -āvī, -ātūrus, *to stay awake*

2nd Conjugation

doceō, docēre, docuī, doctus, *to teach*

doleō, -ēre, -uī, -itūrus, *to be sad*

habeō, -ēre, -uī, -itus, *to have, hold*

iubeō, iubēre, iussī, iussus, *to order, bid*

licet, *it is allowed*

removeō, removēre, remōvī, remōtus, *to remove, move aside*

respondeō, respondēre, respondī, respōnsūrus, *to reply*

rīdeō, rīdēre, rīsī, rīsus, *to laugh (at), smile*

sedeō, sedēre, sēdī, sessūrus, *to sit*

videō, vidēre, vīdī, vīsus, *to see*

3rd Conjugation

dīco, dīcere, dīxī, dictus, *to say, tell*

dūcō, dūcere, dūxī, ductus, *to lead, take, bring*

emō, emere, ēmī, ēmptus, *to buy*

extendō, extendere, extendī, extentus, *to hold out*

extrahō, extrahere, extrāxī, extractus, *to drag out, take out*

mittō, mittere, mīsī, missus, *to send*

petō, petere, petīvī, petītus, *to look for, seek, head for, aim at, attack*

pōnō, pōnere, posuī, positus, *to put, place*

praecurrō, praecurrere, praecurrī, praecursūrus, *to run ahead*

relinquō, relinquere, relīquī, relictus, *to leave behind*

surgō, surgere, surrēxī, surrēctūrus, *to get up, rise*

tremō, tremere, tremuī, *to tremble*

3rd Conjugation -*iō*

capiō, capere, cēpī, captus, *to take, capture*

coniciō, conicere, coniēcī, coniectus, *to throw*

cōnspiciō, cōnspicere, cōnspexī, cōnspectus, *to catch sight of*

effugiō, effugere, effūgī, *to run away, escape*

fugiō, fugere, fūgī, fugitūrus, *to flee*

iaciō, iacere, iēcī, iactus, *to throw*

īnspiciō, īnspicere, īnspexī, īnspectus, *to examine*

olfaciō, olfacere, olfēcī, olfactus, *to catch the scent of, smell, sniff*

4th Conjugation

audiō, -īre, -īvī, -ītus, *to hear, listen to*

ēsuriō, -īre, -īvī, -ītūrus, *to be hungry*

fīniō, fīnīre, fīnīvī, fīnītus, *to finish*

inveniō, invenīre, invēnī, inventus, *to come upon, find*

obdormiō, -īre, -īvī, -ītūrus, *to go to sleep*

pūniō, -īre, -īvī, -ītus, *to punish*

veniō, venīre, vēnī, ventūrus, *to come*

Irregular

eō, īre, iī or **īvī, itūrus,** *to go*

ferō, ferre, tulī, lātus, *to bring, carry*

nōlō, nōlle, nōluī, *to be unwilling, not to wish, refuse*

possum, posse, potuī, *to be able; I can*

sum, esse, fuī, futūrus, *to be*

volō, velle, voluī, *to wish, want, be willing*

PRONOUNS

cui, *to whom, to him, to her*

eī, *to him/her/it*

tibi, *to you, for you*

vōbīs, *to you, for you (pl.)*

PREPOSITIONS

post + acc., *after*

praeter + acc., *except*

ADVERBS

anteā, *previously, before*

attentē, *attentively, closely*

certē, *certainly*

heri, *yesterday*

ita, *thus, so, in this way*

māne, *early in the day, in the morning*

modo, *only*

numquam, *never*

ōlim, *once (upon a time)*

paulisper, *for a short time*

postquam, *after*

sērō, *late*

suprā, *above, on top*

valdē, *very, very much, exceedingly*

vehementer, *very much, violently, hard*

CONJUNCTIONS

enim, *for*

nisi, *unless, if . . . not, except*

quod, *because;* with verbs of feeling, *that*

INTERROGATIVE WORD

Quandō . . . ? *When . . . ?*

MISCELLANEOUS

animum recuperāre, *to regain one's senses, be fully awake*

cubitum īre, *to go to bed*

Estō! *All right!*

hanc, *this*

hī, *these*

hic, haec, hoc, *this*

ille, illa, illud, *that, he, she, it; that famous*

lātrāns, *barking*

licet nobīs, *we are allowed, we may*

manus, *hand*

media nox, *midnight*

Mehercule! *By Hercules! Goodness me!*

melior, *better*

nihil malī, *nothing of a bad thing, there is nothing wrong*

prīmā lūce, *at dawn*

Quid agis? *How are you?*

rem explicāre, *to explain the situation*

sē praecipitāre, *to hurl oneself, rush*

sē rogāre, *to ask oneself, wonder*

sonitus, *sound*

vesperī, *in the evening*

vidētur, *he/she/it seems*

vir optime, *sir*

Activity IVa

Translate into Latin:

1. The Cornelii were sad because (their) carriage was stuck fast in the ditch, but they were happy to approach the inn/they were approaching the inn happily (happy).

_____

_____

2. All the dogs suddenly hurled themselves out of the door. They were wagging their tails happily.

_____

_____

3. "Do you wish to spend the night here, my friends?" asks the fat innkeeper.

_____

_____

4. Aurelia and Cornelia were not able to eat dinner, but the innkeeper ordered slave-women to prepare dinner for Cornelius and Marcus and Sextus.

_____

_____

_____

5. Although the travelers were very tired, they could not sleep in the dirty beds.

_____

_____

6. With a loud laugh, the innkeeper said, "Look, Aurelia and Cornelia, my slaves are bringing other beds. Are you happy now?"

_____

_____

7. "May Marcus and Sextus eat dinner now?" asks Cornelius. "They are very hungry."

_____

_____

8. After dinner Cornelius immediately sent the boys to (their) bedroom.

_____

_____

9. The boys, however, did not want to sleep. They wanted to hear all the stories of the reckless soldier.

_____

_____

10. While two friends were journeying in Greece, they came to a large city.

_____

_____

11. Aulus appeared to his friend in a dream and shouted, "The wicked innkeeper wants to kill me. Help me!"

_____

_____

12. At dawn Septimus found the dead body of his friend in a wagon full of dung.

_____

_____

13. After the boys heard the soldier's story, they were not able to go to sleep.

_____

_____

Activity IVb

Select the item that completes each sentence accurately, based on the readings in _Rome at Last_:

_____ 1. Dum Septimus in vīllā amīcī dormit, Aulus in somnō eī appāruit et clāmāvit,
   a. "Fer auxilium! Mīles mē necāre parat."
   b. "Fer auxilium! Caupō mē necāre parat."
   c. "Abī! Tū es scelestus."
   d. "Prīmā lūce nōbīs exīre licet."

_____ 2. Mediā nocte sub lectō Sextī erant
   a. fēlēs et canis.
   b. fēlēs obēsa et mūs mortuus.
   c. fēlēs mortua et mūs sēmisomnus.
   d. mīles quīdam et caupō mortuus.

_____ 3. Cornēliī in caupōnam intrāvērunt quod
   a. Marcus et Sextus ēsuriēbant.
   b. Aurēlia dēfessa erat.
   c. raeda in fossā haerēbat immōbilis.
   d. iam lūcēbat.

_____ 4. Cornēlia nōn cēnāre sed
   a. redīre ad vīllam vult.
   b. tantum cubitum īre vult.
   c. ad mediam noctem vigilāre vult.
   d. fābulam mīlitis audīre vult.

_____ 5. Duo canēs ē iānuā caupōnae sē praecipitant et
   a. Cornēlia perterrita fugit.
   b. Marcus ad canem currit.
   c. puerī lacrimant.
   d. Cornēlius ipse nihil facit.

Activity IVc

ACROSS

2. Heri ego et Marcus prīmā lūce _____. (got up)

7. Pater _____ tacēbat, sed tandem, "Estō!" inquit. (for a short time)

8. "Servī meī," inquit caupō, "alium lectum _____ parāvērunt." (for you)

9. "Ego in hanc caupōnam," inquit Aurēlia, "invīta _____." (have entered)

11. Dum Septimus dormit, Aulus in somnō _____ appāruit. (to him)

12. Ubi plaustrum invēnit, Septimus _____ remōvit. (the dung)

14. Caupōnem cēnam bonam parāre _____. (they ordered)

16. _____ raedārius raedam agēbat? (How)

19. Geta cistam in raedam _____. (was throwing)

22. "Ō Apollodōre," exclāmat Eucleidēs, "canēs _____!" (call back)

26. Tabellāriī ad omnēs Italiae partēs _____. (were going)

27. "In meā caupōnā," inquit caupō, "_____ semper bona est." (dinner)

28. Nōs raedam Cornēliānam ē fossā lentē _____. (were pulling out)

DOWN

1. "Ōlim in meā caupōnā," inquit caupō, "pernoctāvit etiam _____ prīncipis." (envoy)

2. Caupō stercus _____ coniēcit. (on top)

3. "Prope Viam Appiam," inquit caupō, "nūlla caupōna _____ est." (better)

4. "Nihil malī," inquit Septimus, "_____ modo fuit." (dream)

5. "Ego et Marcus nōn _____," inquit Cornēlia, "quod canēs nōn timēmus." (are . . . fleeing)

6. "Multī _____," inquit caupō, "ad meam caupōnam venīre solent." (travelers)

7. Vōs auxilium in hāc caupōnā _____. (have sought)

13. "In Asiam īre volō," inquit Sextus. "Ibi _____ nūllum est perīculum." (for)

15. "Ego statim ē lectō _____," inquit Sextus. (got up)

17. Viātōrēs multa dē perīculīs viārum _____. (say)

18. "Ad illam _____ īre nōlō," clāmat Aurēlia. (inn)

20. _____ canum erant longae. (The tails)

21. Cornēlia nōn iam _____, sed tantum cubitum īre vult. (is hungry)

23. "Ego sum _____ dēfessa," inquit Aurēlia. (very)

24. Cornēlia _____ ad canēs extendit. (hand)

25. "Nōnne audīvistī," rogat mīles, "illam fābulam _____ caupōne scelestō nārrātam?" (about)

Activity 22a

Write the dative singular and plural for each of the following nouns (the regular dictionary forms, i.e., the nominative and genitive singular, are supplied):

	Dative Singular	*Dative Plural*
1. viātor, viātōris	_____	_____
2. fābula, fābulae	_____	_____
3. ager, agrī	_____	_____
4. auxilium, auxiliī	_____	_____
5. lectus, lectī	_____	_____
6. homō, hominis	_____	_____
7. lēgātus, lēgātī	_____	_____
8. hospes, hospitis	_____	_____
9. vir, virī	_____	_____
10. iter, itineris	_____	_____

Activity 22b

Give the dative forms of each of the following adjectives and pronouns. For adjectives, give the dative forms in the gender indicated by the nominative singular form:

	Dative Singular	*Dative Pural*
1. nocturnus	_____	_____
2. vōs		_____
3. is	_____	
4. obēsa	_____	_____
5. incolume	_____	_____
6. tū	_____	
7. ea (she)	_____	
8. ego	_____	
9. id	_____	
10. sordidum	_____	_____
11. eī (they)		_____
12. nōs		_____
13. ea (they)		_____
14. omnis	_____	_____
15. eae		_____

Activity 22c

To whom . . . ? To what . . . ? *Cui* . . . ? *Quibus* . . . ? Answer the following questions with words in the dative case, keeping to the story in Chapter 22:

1. Cui servī cistās Cornēliōrum trādidērunt? _____

2. Cui Sextus mīlitis fābulam nārrābat? _____

3. Quibus Eucleidēs mandāta dabat? _____

4. Quibus Cornēlius clāmābat? _____

5. Cui Sextus omnia dē mūre mortuō explicāvit? _____

6. Cui Cornēlius mīlitis fābulam nārrāvit? _____

7. Cui appropinquābant Cornēliī? _____

8. Quibus nōn licet intrā urbem sepulcra habēre? _____

9. Cui Marcus nihil respondit? _____

10. Cui Cornēlius omnia explicāvit? _____

Activity 22d

Keeping to the story in Chapter 22, answer the following questions with complete Latin sentences:

1. When did the carriage driver pull the carriage out of the ditch?

   _____

2. With whose help did he pull it out?

   _____

3. To what place did he move the carriage?

   _____

4. What did the Cornelii do when they went out of the inn?

   _____

5. Where was the innkeeper standing when he said goodbye?

   _____

6. When did Sextus explain everything to Marcus about the dead mouse?

   _____

7. When did the boys catch sight of a huge building?

   _____

8. Who was living in the building?

   _____

9. Who was Messalla Corvinus?

   _____

10. Where are Romans not allowed to have tombs?

_____

11. Whose was the other tomb?

_____

12. What did Marcus shout when he saw Rome?

_____

13. Who is Titus?

_____

14. Who sent a letter to him?

_____

15. Who carried the letter?

_____

16. Who will welcome the Cornelii?

_____

17. Where will he welcome them?

_____

Activity 22e
Use an English dictionary and find meanings for the following:

1. uxorious _____

2. advent _____

3. Advent _____

4. sepulcher a. _____

           b. _____

5. mandate a. _____

           b. _____

           _____

           c. _____

_____

Activity 22f
From what Latin verb does the dative case get its name? _____
Explain the relationship between the meaning of this verb and the concept of the dative case:

_____

_____

CHAPTER 23

AT THE PORTA CAPENA

Activity 23a
Complete these statements:

1. Regular verbs of the _____ and _____ conjugations have future tense endings different from regular verbs of the _____ and _____ conjugations.

2. The irregular verb **īre** uses the same future tense endings as do the _____ and _____ conjugations.

3. The irregular verbs **velle**, **nōlle**, and **ferre** use the same future tense endings as do the _____ and _____ conjugations.

4. Except in the 1st person singular, the future tense of a 3rd conjugation verb like **mittere** is identical to the _____ tense of a 2nd conjugation verb like **habēre**.

Activity 23b
Circle the future tense verb in each pair:

1. manēs, sūmēs
2. movēmus, agēmus
3. erit, erat
4. accidet, licet
5. poterunt, potuērunt
6. iubētis, cadētis
7. iacent, iacient
8. poteris, poterās
9. ībat, ībit
10. volet, voluit
11. eram, cōnstituam
12. reprehendent, respondent

Activity 23c
Change to future tense, keeping the same person and number:

1. dēscendunt _____
2. exspectat _____
3. vīs _____
4. pluit _____
5. est _____
6. narrāmus _____
7. excipiunt _____
8. videō _____
9. possumus _____
10. eunt _____
11. condūcō _____
12. dormītis _____
13. fers _____
14. sunt _____
15. nōlumus _____
16. cōnstituit _____

Activity 23d

Fill in the blanks with Latin words to match the English cues:

1. Cīvēs _____ _____ currēbant. (this way and that)

2. Raeda ad portam _____ manēbit. (during the day)

3. _____ erant clāmōrēs mercātōrum. (On all sides)

4. Titus līberōs _____ _____ _____ salūtāvit.
(with very great joy)

5. Ubi _____ advēnērunt, Cornēliī ē raedā dēscendērunt. (there)

6. Titus _____ lectīcās condūxit. (first)

7. _____ portam erat aquaeductus. (Above)

8. Eucleidēs et puerī _____ Portam Capēnam stābant. (outside)

9. "_____ caupōnam vīdimus!" clāmāvit Sextus. (But)

10. "_____ Circum Maximum vīsitābimus?" rogat Marcus. (When)

11. Marcus _____ cīvium in viā spectābat. (the multitude)

12. "_____ nōs domum ferent," inquit Cornēlius. (Litter-bearers)

Activity 23e

Fill in the blanks with Latin words to match the English cues. Be sure to put the Latin words in the correct form in the sentence:

1. _____ per Portam Capēnam ībant. (The merchants)

2. Titus tamen in _____ sedēbat. (a litter)

3. Prope portam Marcus _____ servōrum vīdit. (a crowd)

4. Cornēlius Aurēliam et Cornēliam _____ dūxit. (home)

5. _____ _____

_____ vidēbunt puerī. (Many wonderful things)

6. Marcī pater togam _____ induit. (of manhood)

7. Cornēlius ad _____ celeriter ībat. (the Senate House)

8. Marcus _____ fābulās valdē amābat. (such)

9. Vidēsne _____ urbis ingentēs? (the walls)

10. Sextus saepe _____ est. (stupid)

11. Puerī, quamquam sordidī fuērunt, _____ nōn

_____ . (did . . . wash themselves)

12. Māter in cubiculō _____

_____ _____ . (rested)

Activity 23f
Translate into Latin:

The carriage of the Cornelii was approaching the gate of the city.

_____

_____

CORNĒLIUS: Look! I can see the Porta Capena. Soon we will be in the city.

_____

MARCUS: Who will welcome us there, father? Will we go home immediately?

_____

CORNĒLIUS: First we will greet your uncle, who will certainly be waiting for us.

_____

Then I will hire litter-bearers because it will be necessary to take your mother and Cornelia home.

_____

_____

But you and Sextus will be able to remain with Titus.

_____

MARCUS: Hurray! Will he take us to the Circus Maximus?

_____

CORNĒLIUS: Perhaps, but you will also want to visit the Forum and the Senate House.

_____

_____

Titus will tell you many things about the buildings of Rome.

_____

_____

SEXTUS: I'll be very glad when we see Rome.

_____

_____

Activity 23g

In each sentence give the correct future tense form of the verb(s) in parentheses:

1. Ego, sī hīc _____ , certē miser _____ . (manēre) (esse)

2. Servī cistās in cubiculum _____ . (ferre)

3. Ubi tū crās _____ , Tite? Nōnne tū in urbem _____ ?
   (esse) (dēscendere)

4. Nōs patrī rem explicāre nōn _____ . (posse)

5. Ego in lectīcā _____ , et lectīcāriī mē domum _____ .
   (cōnsīdere) (portāre)

6. Senātor ad Cūriam crās _____ . (īre)

7. Tū togam virīlem _____ . (induere)

8. Aurēlia et Cornēlia domum redīre _____ . (velle)

9. Sī Titus ad Portam Capēnam _____ , nōs excipere

   _____ . (manēre) (posse)

10. Nōnne tū Circum Maximum vīsitāre _____ ? (velle)

Activity 23h

**Give the Latin word to which each of the following English words is related, and
give the meaning of the English word:**

	Latin Word	Meaning of the English Word
1. agent	_____	_____
2. agile	_____	_____
3. agenda	_____	_____
4. domestic	_____	_____
5. miracle	_____	_____
6. stupefy	_____	_____
7. prime	_____	_____
8. turbulent	_____	_____
9. mercantile	_____	_____
10. acquiescent	_____	_____

CHAPTER 24

ALWAYS TOMORROW

Activity 24a
Fill in the blanks as your teacher reads the story aloud:

Simulac Titus et puerī et Eucleidēs urbem per Portam Capēnam

_____ , clāmāvit Sextus, "Quid nōs prīmum faciēmus?

Quō _____ ? Vīsitābimusne — ?"

"Quō tū nōs dūcēs, patrue?" interpellāvit Marcus. "Vidēbimusne Cūriam et Forum?

5   Sextus multa dē Rōmā _____ et audīvit et nunc, patrue, omnia vidēre vult."

Titus, "Tacēte! Tacēte!" inquit. "Forum crās _____ . Crās,

Eucleidēs, tibi _____ puerōs eō dūcere. Tum erit satis temporis.
Hodiē tamen, puerī, vōs domum per urbem dūcam et omnia in itinere vōbīs dēmōnstrābō."

Iam _____ ad Circum Maximum, quī nōn procul aberat. Stupuit

10   Sextus ubi _____ Circī Maximī vīdit. Marcus quoque stupuit,

quamquam Circum anteā _____ . Stupuit Titus,

_____ nōn mōle, sed silentiō Circī.

"Ēheu! Ēheu!" inquit Titus. "Hodiē Circus est _____ .

Tribus diēbus tamen prīnceps ipse, Titus Flāvius Vespasiānus, _____
15   magnificōs faciet."

"Nōnne tū nōs eō _____ ?" rogāvit Marcus.

"Ēheu! Ego nōn poterō vōs dūcere," inquit Titus. "_____
Eucleidēs vōs dūcet."

"Minimē!" respondit Sextus. "_____ , nōn lūdōs amat Eucleidēs."

20   "Agite, puerī!" interpellāvit Titus. "Nunc _____

Montem Palātīnum et Forum intrābimus ad _____ Tiberiī.
Ibi fortasse patrī tuō occurrēmus, Marce. Mox senātōrēs ē Cūriā exībunt."

Itaque Circum _____ et Palātīnum circumiērunt. Titus in itinere

mōnstrāvit puerīs mīra aedificia quae prīncipēs in Palātīnō _____ .

25   Tandem ad arcum Tiberiī advēnērunt, iam labōre et _____ dēfessī.
"Hic est arcus," inquit Titus, "quem —"

"Omnia vidēre _____ crās," interpellāvit Cornēlius, quī eō ipsō

tempore ad arcum ē Cūriā advēnerat. "Cum ad Forum crās _____ ,

Eucleidēs omnia vōbīs explicābit. Iam sērō est. Agite! Iam domum _____ ."

Activity 24b

Change the following verbs from present to pluperfect tense, keeping the same person and number:

1. appārent _____
2. removēmus _____
3. adiuvās _____
4. dat _____
5. sūmitis _____
6. is _____

7. ferunt _____
8. agimus _____
9. cōnspiciō _____
10. iubēs _____
11. pōnitis _____
12. sum _____

Activity 24c

Change the following verbs from present to future perfect tense, keeping the same person and number:

1. aedificāmus _____
2. occurritis _____
3. vult _____
4. stupēs _____
5. fīnit _____
6. possumus _____
7. colit _____

8. nōlō _____
9. cōgitant _____
10. ferunt _____
11. cōnspicimus _____
12. induis _____
13. īs _____
14. conicit _____

Activity 24d

Supply the requested words in the following sentences:

1. Iam puerī urbem _____ . Marcus, "Quandō pater ad

   Cūriam _____ ?" inquit. (had entered) (will go)

2. Puerī, sī _____ Circum Maximum, laetī domum ībunt.
   (they see/they will have seen)

3. Sī puerī Cornēliō in Forō _____ , eōs domum dūcet.
   (meet/will have met)

4. Sextus, quī numquam anteā Rōmae _____ , attonitus erat. (had been)

5. Stupuit Sextus ubi Circum vīdit quod numquam anteā tāle aedificium

   _____ . (he had seen)

6. Sī sērō domum _____ , pater valdē īrātus erit. (we
   arrive/we will have arrived)

7. Cum in urbem crās _____ , Sexte, Circum Maximum
   iterum vidēbis. (you descend/you will have descended)

(continued)

8. Nisi prīmā lūce _____ , puerī, vōs in urbem nōn dūcam.
   (you get up/you will have gotten up)

9. Puerī cubitum īre nōlēbant quod fābulam dē Aulī morte _____ .
   (had heard)

10. Ille caupō, sī Aulus in caupōnam _____ , eum certē necābit.
    (enters/will have entered)

Activity 24e
Translate into Latin:

1. The boys, who had left the Circus Maximus and gone around the Palatine Hill, descended to the Forum.

   _____

   _____

2. They were tired from the labor and heat.

   _____

3. Near the arch of Tiberius they met Cornelius.

   _____

4. Cornelius had already taken the boys home. They were tired. "Tomorrow," said Cornelius, "you will see all the wonderful buildings in the city."

   _____

   _____

5. "In three days, when you and Eucleides enter/will have entered the Circus Maximus, you will see the games."

   _____

   _____

Activity 24f
Give meanings for the following English words. Where possible, show how the meaning of the English word is related to that of the Latin word from which it comes. Use an English dictionary as necessary:

1. occur   a. _____

          b. _____

2. library _____

3. ludicrous _____

4. edifice _____

5. astonished _____

6. palace _____

   _____

VOCABULARY FOR REVIEW

NOUNS

1st Declension

Cūria, -ae, f., *Senate House*

habēnae, -ārum, f. pl., *reins*

lectīca, -ae, f., *litter*

turba, -ae, f., *crowd, mob*

2nd Declension

Circus Maximus, -ī, m., *Circus Maximus (a stadium in Rome)*

gaudium, -ī, n., *joy*

lectīcārius, -ī, m., *litter-bearer*

liber, librī, m., *book*

lūdī, -ōrum, m. pl., *games*

mandātum, -ī, n., *order, instruction*

mūrus, -ī, m., *wall*

patruus, -ī, m., *uncle*

sepulcrum, -ī, n., *tomb*

3rd Declension

hominēs, hominum, m. pl., *people*

imber, imbris, m., *rain*

labor, labōris, m., *work, toil*

mercātor, mercātōris, m., *merchant*

mōlēs, mōlis, f., *mass, huge bulk*

mōns, montis, gen. pl., **montium**, m., *mountain, hill*

multitūdō, multitūdinis, f., *crowd*

ōrātor, ōrātōris, m., *orator, speaker*

pōns, pontis, gen. pl., **pontium**, m., *bridge*

quiēs, quiētis, f., *rest*

terror, terrōris, m., *terror, fear*

ADJECTIVES

1st and 2nd Declension

attonitus, -a, -um, *astonished, astounded*

clausus, -a, -um, *shut, closed*

magnificus, -a, -um, *magnificent*

maximus, -a, -um, *greatest, very great, very large*

mīrus, -a, -um, *wonderful, marvelous, strange*

nocturnus, -a, -um, *happening during the night*

Palātīnus, -a, -um, *Palatine, belonging to the Palatine Hill*

rīmōsus, -a, -um, *full of cracks, leaky*

stultus, -a, -um, *stupid, foolish*

tantus, -a, -um, *so great, such a big*

vester, vestra, vestrum, *your* (pl.)

3rd Declension

immemor, immemoris + gen., *forgetful*

ingēns, ingentis, *huge*

tālis, -is -e, *such, like this, of this kind*

virīlis, -is, -e, *of manhood*

VERBS

1st Conjugation

aedificō, -āre, -āvī, -ātus, *to build*

dēmōnstrō, -āre, -āvī, -ātus, *to show*

mōnstrō, -āre, -āvī, -ātus, *to show*

stō, stāre, stetī, statūrus, *to stand*

vīsitō, -āre, -āvī, -ātus, *to visit*

2nd Conjugation

admoveō, admovēre, admōvī, admōtus, *to move toward*

caveō, cavēre, cāvī, cautus, *to be careful, watch out for, beware*

licet, licēre, licuit + dat., *it is allowed*

maneō, manēre, mānsī, mānsūrus, *to remain, stay, wait*

moveō, movēre, mōvī, mōtus, *to move*

stupeō, -ēre, -uī, *to be amazed, gape*

3rd Conjugation

agō, agere, ēgī, āctus, *to do, drive*

ascendō, ascendere, ascendī, ascēnsūrus, *to climb, climb into (a carriage)*

cadō, cadere, cedidī, cāsūrus, *to fall*

colō, colere, coluī, cultus, *to cultivate*

condūcō, condūcere, condūxī, conductus, *to hire*

cōnsīdō, cōnsīdere, cōnsēdī, *to sit down*

cōnstituō, cōnstituere, cōnstituī, cōnstitūtus, *to decide*

currō, currere, cucurrī, cursūrus, *to run*

dēscendō, dēscendere, dēscendī, dēscēnsūrus, *to come/go down, climb down*

discēdō, discēdere, discessī, discessūrus, *to go away, depart*

induō, induere, induī, indūtus, *to put on*

legō, legere, lēgī, lēctus, *to read*

occurrō, occurrere, occurrī, occursūrus + dat., *to meet*

pluit, pluere, pluit, *it rains, is raining*

quiēscō, quiēscere, quiēvī, quiētūrus, *to rest, keep quiet*

scrībō, scrībere, scrīpsī, scrīptus, *to write*

sūmō, sūmere, sūmpsī, sūmptus, *to take, take up, pick out*

trādō, trādere, trādidī, trāditus, *to hand over*

3rd Conjugation -iō

excipiō, excipere, excēpī, exceptus, *to welcome, receive, catch*

faciō, facere, fēcī, factus, *to make, do*

4th Conjugation

adveniō, advenīre, advēnī, adventūrus, *to reach, arrive (at)*

Irregular

circumeō, circumīre, circumiī or **circumīvī, circumitus**, *to go around*

exeō, exīre, exiī or **exīvī, exitūrus**, *to go out*

redeō, redīre, rediī or **redīvī, reditūrus**, *to return, go back*

PRONOUNS

Cuius . . . ? *Whose . . . ?* (sing.)
eī, eae, ea, *they*
eīs, *to them*
quem, *whom, which, that* (sing.)

PREPOSITIONS

extrā + acc., *outside*
intrā + acc., *inside*
suprā + acc., *above*

ADVERBS

bene, *well*
eō, *there, to that place*
hūc illūc, *here and there, this way and that*
illūc, *there, to that place*
interdiū, *during the day, by day*
prīmum, *first, at first*
satis, *enough*
undique, *on all sides, from all sides*
vix, *scarcely, with difficulty*

CONJUNCTIONS

at, *but*
atque, *and, also*
cum, *when*
simulac, *as soon as*

MISCELLANEOUS

aestus, *heat*
aquaeductus, *aqueduct*
arcus, *arch*
Cavē!/Cavēte! *Be careful! Watch out for . . . ! Beware!*
domō, *from home*
domum, *homeward, home*
domus, *house*
exstāns, exstantis, *standing out, towering*
satis temporis, *enough time*
sē parāre, *to prepare oneself, get ready*
sē quiētī dare, *to rest*
strepitus, *noise, clattering*

Activity Va
Translate into Latin:

1. Although the slaves had seen the chests yesterday, they could not find them today.

   _____

   _____

2. On the journey Sextus will explain to Marcus everything about the dead mouse, and Cornelius will tell Aurelia a story about a wicked innkeeper who killed a guest.

   _____

   _____

   _____

3. Near the Porta Capena the Cornelii will find Titus, the children's uncle, because Cornelius sent him a letter and explained everything to him.

   _____

   _____

   _____

   _____

4. Titus will have hired litter-bearers who will carry Cornelius, Aurelia, and Cornelia home.

   _____

   _____

5. While Aurelia and Cornelia rested, Cornelius went to the Senate House.

   _____

   _____

6. Sextus was able to see the huge Circus Maximus towering above the city walls.

   _____

   _____

7. Although Eucleides loves books, not the games, he will take the boys to the Circus Maximus tomorrow.

   _____

   _____

8. Cornelius, who had come out of the Senate House, met the boys at the arch of Tiberius. "It's late. Come on! We will go home now," he said to them.

   _____

   _____

   _____

Activity Vb

Fill in the spaces at the right with translations of the English at the left. When you are finished, copy the circled letters in order and you will discover a Latin *sententia*. Write its meaning below:

1. they will build   __ __ __ __ Ⓞ __ __ __ __ __ __ __
2. outside   __ __ __ __ Ⓞ
3. so great (m. nom. sing.)   __ __ __ Ⓞ __ __ __
4. I shall meet   __ __ __ __ __ __ Ⓞ __
5. your (pl.) (f. nom.)   Ⓞ __ __ __ __ __
6. scarcely   __ __ Ⓞ __ __
7. she had done (**agō**)   __ __ __ __ Ⓞ __
8. hill (nom.)   Ⓞ __ __ __
9. books (nom.)   __ Ⓞ __ __ __
10. astonished (m. nom. sing.)   __ __ __ Ⓞ __ __ __ __ __
11. you (sing.) will arrive   __ __ Ⓞ __ __ __ __
12. you (pl.) will leave   __ Ⓞ __ __ __ __ __ __
13. they will carry   __ __ __ Ⓞ __ __
14. I will hear   __ __ Ⓞ __ __
15. to go around   __ __ __ __ __ __ __ __ Ⓞ __
16. they will put on   __ __ __ __ __ Ⓞ __
17. they had brought   Ⓞ __ __ __ __ __ __ __ __

Copy circled letters here: __ __ __ __ __ __ __ __ __ __ __ __ __ __ __ __ __ .

Meaning of *sententia*: _____

Activity Vc

Find and circle the Latin words for the English words listed to the right. Words may go in a horizontal, vertical, or diagonal direction, but they do not go backward:

1. tomb
2. this way and that
3. inside
4. during the day
5. such
6. there, to that place
7. crowd, mob
8. so great, such a big
9. on all sides
10. as soon as
11. your (pl.)
12. well
13. order, instruction
14. bridge
15. and

```
e o b s t f x h m l t a l i s
a d m s e e g u r b q u a m f
n t a n t p v c t p u x r p d
p o n z t a u i z a y n z b l
o u d b e k e l g i n i d k a
e q a v p r o l c q n t e i y
i n t e r d i u i r x v u b q
n h u s y d n c n g u f c s z
t z m t u v t x t z t m r b c
r a l a q n r y i l l u c u v
a c q t s f d m r p m a t q e
f e r q t a l i d p o n s t s
o k h u c i l l q t s b u l t
g r b e n s n o d u t b e n e
s i m u l a c n h x e i k v r
```

Activity Vd

ACROSS

3. at first
8. mountain, hill (nom. sing.)
10. for a long time
11. coachman (dat. sing.)
14. they will drive
15. merchant (dat. sing.)
16. reins (nom. pl.)
18. put on! (imperative sing.)
21. I will come
22. you (sing.) are amazed
24. she gives
26. he is going
28. they will go
30. noise (nom. sing.)
33. outside
34. she had handed over
36. wall (acc. sing.)

DOWN

1. when, with
2. you (pl.) had seen
3. through, along
4. I will go
5. mass, huge bulk (acc. sing.)
6. we will take care of
7. uncle (nom. sing.)
9. enough
12. threshing floor (nom. sing.)
13. huge (nom. sing. masc.)
15. it remains
17. I had heard
19. and
20. stupid! (vocative sing.)
21. scarcely
23. he will be able
25. from
27. they will be
29. I will hand over
31. I will prepare
32. he will take up
35. you (nom. sing.)

CHAPTER 25

FIRST MORNING IN ROME

Activity 25a

Fill in the blanks as your teacher reads the story aloud:

Iam diēs erat. Magnus erat _____ in urbe. Servī ad Forum

magnō _____ onera ferēbant. Undique clāmor et

strepitus! Sed nihil clāmōris, nihil _____ ad Marcum

pervēnit. In lectō stertēbat, nam dēfessus erat. Sextus quoque in lectō manēbat sed

5 _____ nōn poterat. Clāmōribus et strepitū

_____ , iam cōgitābat dē omnibus

_____ quās Titus heri nārrāverat. "Quid hodiē

vidēbimus? Cornēliusne nōs in Forum dūcet? Ego certē Forum et Cūriam et senātōrēs

vidēre volō."

10 Intereā Eucleidēs, quī prīmā lūce exierat, iam domum _____ .

Statim cubiculum puerōrum petīvit et, "Eho, puerī!" inquit. "Cūr nōndum surrēxistis?

_____ duās hōrās ego surrēxī. Quod novum librum emere

volēbam, in Argīlētum māne dēscendī ad _____ quandam ubi

in _____ nōmina multōrum _____

15 vidēre potes. Catullus, Flaccus—"

At puerī celeriter interpellāvērunt quod Eucleidēs, ut _____

sciēbant, semper _____ novī docēre volēbat. "Quid in viīs vīdistī?"

Eucleidēs, "Nihil," inquit, "nisi miserum hominem _____

oppressum. Bovēs lapidēs _____ in plaustrō trahēbant ad novum

20 aedificium quod Caesar prope Domum Auream cōnficit. Illud aedificium est ingēns

_____ et mox prīnceps lūdōs ibi faciet. Sī bonī puerī

_____ , fortasse ad lūdōs ībitis."

Activity 25b
Fill in the blanks with the proper forms of the noun *strepitus, -ūs* (m.):

1. Sextus magnum _____ in viā audīvit.

2. Nihil _____ in domō erat.

3. Plaustra magnō cum _____ nocte per viās onera ferēbant.

4. Marcus dormiēbat et stertēbat. Magnōs _____ canum in viā nōn audīvit.

5. Tandem Marcus multīs clāmōribus et magnīs _____ excitātus ē lectō surrēxit.

6. Ingēns _____ aurīgārum puerōs dormientēs excitāvit.

7. _____ multōrum vehiculōrum nocte in viīs Rōmae erant.

Activity 25c
Fill in the blanks with the proper forms of the noun *rēs, reī* (f.):

1. Sextus Marcō _____ explicāvit.

2. Quās _____ hodiē vidēre vultis?

3. Servī multīs _____ plaustra onerābant.

4. Plaustrum erat plēnum multārum _____ .

5. Multae _____ nōs in urbe nocte vexābant.

6. Pecūnia est _____ omnium optima.

7. Quae est causa huius _____ malae?

8. Eucleidēs librum dē _____ rūsticā legit.

onerō, -āre, -āvī, -ātus,
to load

Activity 25d
Give English translations of the following Latin phrases that use the partitive genitive:

1. satis temporis _____

2. nihil temporis _____

3. multum temporis _____

4. satis pecūniae _____

5. nihil pecūniae _____

6. multum pecūniae _____

7. multum strepitūs _____

8. multum clāmōris _____

9. multum tumultūs _____

Activity 25e
Use an English dictionary and find meanings for the following:

1. rebus _____

_____

2. tabernacle a. _____

b. _____

c. _____

_____

3. tumult _____

4. tumultuous _____

5. tavern _____

6. docile _____

7. docent _____

8. indoctrinate _____

_____

CHAPTER 26 · A GRIM LESSON

Activity 26a

In the left-hand column, write the proper form of *hic, haec, hoc* to go with each noun; in the right-hand column write the proper form of *ille, illa, illud* to go with each noun. Be sure to choose forms of *hic* and *ille* that agree with the nouns in gender, case, and number. The nouns used are in the box at the right:

cēna, -ae, f.
oculus, -ī, m.
aedificium, -ī, n.
praedō, praedōnis, m.
urbs, urbis, f.
nōmen, nōminis, n.
arcus, -ūs, m.
rēs, reī, f.

hic, haec, hoc

1. _____ aedificium
2. _____ praedōnem
3. _____ rēs (acc.)
4. _____ arcū
5. _____ oculī (nom.)
6. _____ urbium
7. _____ cēnae (gen.)
8. _____ praedō
9. _____ nōmen
10. _____ rē
11. _____ urbī
12. _____ aedificiī
13. _____ arcuum
14. _____ oculō
15. _____ aedificia

ille, illa, illud

16. _____ cēnae (nom.)
17. _____ praedōnēs (acc.)
18. _____ urbs
19. _____ oculum
20. _____ urbis
21. _____ aedificiīs
22. _____ nōmine
23. _____ oculōs
24. _____ praedōnibus
25. _____ rērum
26. _____ cēnam
27. _____ praedōnēs (nom.)
28. _____ oculōrum
29. _____ arcuī
30. _____ oculus

Activity 26b

Fill in each blank with the proper form of *hic* or *ille*, according to the English cues:

1. "Cavē _____ praedōnēs!" clāmāvit ūnus ex

   _____ cīvibus. (those) (these)

2. Pater _____ puerī est _____ senātor. (of this) (that)

3. Cīvēs pecūniam in _____ viā _____ mercātōrī dabant. (this) (to that)

4. _____ praedōnēs certē _____ bona arripient. (These) (those)

5. Eucleidēs _____ rēs _____ puerīs nārrābat. (these) (to those)

(continued)

6. In postibus _____ tabernārum _____ nōmina invēnimus. (of those) (these)

7. Puerī in _____ urbem sine _____ custōde nōn dēscendent. (that) (this)

8. _____ diē caupō scelestus _____ hospitem necāvit. (On that) (this)

9. Aurēlia neque _____ caupōnam neque _____ caupōnem amat. (that) (that)

10. Ego _____ gladium _____ manū strīnxī. (this) (this)

Activity 26c
Fill in the blanks with Latin words to match the English cues:

1. Praedōnēs in viīs viātōrēs _____ exspectant. (sometimes)

2. Marcus _____ - _____ ibi stābat immōbilis. (moved by fear)

3. _____ puerī ad Circum ībunt. (On the following day)

4. Eucleidēs multa dē _____ urbis nārrābat. (the noise)

5. Cornēlia ad Forum cum _____ - _____ ībit. (this guard)

6. In urbe _____ - _____ vidēbitis. (those arches)

7. Cornēlius _____ - _____ uxōrī suae explicābat. (this situation)

8. _____ Marcī sunt clausī. (Eyes)

9. Aurēlia īrāta fuit ubi in ātriō _____ - _____ cōnspexit. (that mud)

10. _____ - _____ servī sub arboribus quiēscēbant. (On that day)

11. Sextus _____ suās lavāre nōn vult. (hands)

12. Post _____ - _____ ad vīllam rūsticam redībimus. (many days)

13. Servī cum clāmōribus et _____ onera ferēbant. (smiles)

14. Cīvēs ab urbe _____ - _____ suīs discēdere nōlunt. (without . . . goods)

15. Quid est causa _____ - _____ ? (of this uproar)

16. Crās Marcus _____ manēbit. (at home)

17. Cornēlius est dominus _____ - _____ . (of that country house)

18. Nōlī _____ vehiculum in _____ urbem agere! (that) (this)

Activity 26d
Change all singular nouns, pronouns, adjectives, and verbs to plural:

1. Hoc mandātum senātūs illī cīvī dabō.

   _____

2. Frāter huius senātōris prope arcum illam raedam exspectāverat.

   _____

   _____

3. Audīvistīne illum strepitum in hāc viā?

   _____

4. Hic servus ad forum magnō tumultū illud onus ferēbat.

   _____

5. Hanc rem meā manū fēcī; sine auxiliō servī labōrāre poteram.

   _____

   _____

6. Pater fīlium manum lavāre iubēbit.

   _____

Activity 26e
Give the Latin word to which each group of English words is related; then give the meaning of each English word. Use an English dictionary, as needed.

Latin Word	English Word	Meaning of the English Word
1. _____	terrain	_____
	terrestrial	_____
	territory	_____
	terrarium	_____
		_____
		_____
	inter	_____
2. _____	innocent	_____
	innocuous	_____
	noxious	_____
	obnoxious	_____
3. _____	aperture	_____
	overt	_____
	pert	_____

Activity 26f

Give the meaning of each of these Latin expressions used in English. Consult an English dictionary as necessary.

1. sine die _____

_____

2. sine prole _____

_____

3. terra firma _____

_____

4. terra incognita _____

_____

Is the English word "inoculate" derived from the Latin word *nocēre* or from the Latin word *oculus*? Look up "inoculate" in an English dictionary and explain its derivation:

_____

_____

_____

_____

_____

_____

CHAPTER 27 | A VISIT TO THE RACES

Activity 27a

Answer in full Latin sentences these questions based on the story in Chapter 27:

1. Quō licet puerīs īre hodiē?

_____

2. Quī cum puerīs ībunt?

_____

3. Cūr Circus hodiē nōn clausus est?

_____

4. Cūr puerī statim discēdere nōn possunt?

_____

5. Quid audiunt puerī, ubi Circō appropinquant?

_____

6. Quālis est turba?

_____

7. Ubi Marcus sedēre vult? Cūr?

_____

8. Cūr Eucleidēs ibi sedēre nōn vult?

_____

9. Quis venetīs favet?

_____

10. Quid fēcit aurīga Marcī?

_____

11. Quōmodo aurīgae equōs agunt?

_____

12. Quid semper clāmant spectātōrēs?

_____

13. Quī vīcērunt?

_____

14. Cūr domum redīre necesse est?

_____

15. Cūr nōn vult redīre Sextus?

_____

Basilica Iūlia   *Arcus Tiberiī*   *Cūria*   *Basilica Aemilia*   *Aquaeductus*

Activity 27b

In the description of chariot racing on the first page of Chapter 27, find the Latin word(s) corresponding to each of the following English terms and write them on the lines provided:

1. four-horse chariots: _____

2. white cloth dropped as the starting signal: _____

3. race-course: _____

4. chariot races: _____

5. turning posts: _____

6. huge stadium for racing in Rome: _____

7. holidays on which races were held: _____

8. barrier running down the center of the course: _____

9. "Reds": _____ "Whites": _____

   "Greens": _____ "Blues": _____

10. teams or companies: _____

Activity 27c

Fill in the blanks with Latin words to match the English cues:

1. Hodiē ad Circum Maximum īre _____

   _____ . (the boys will be allowed)

2. Eucleidēs cum puerīs et Cornēliā _____ . (will go)

3. Puerī statim discēdere _____ _____ ,

   quod Cornēlia adhūc _____ . (were not able) (was sleeping)

4. Puerī īrātī fuērunt, quod Cornēlia nōndum _____ . (had gotten up)

5. Ubi _____ appropinquant, magnum

   _____ audiunt. (Circus) (noise)

6. "Turba _____ est ingēns!" clāmat Cornēlia. (of spectators)

7. "Ibi omnia vidēre _____ , Marce," inquit Cornēlia. (you will be able)

8. "Puerī, _____ _____ prope

   curriculum!" inquit Eucleidēs. (don't sit)

9. "Prope curriculum cōnsīdere _____

   _____ ," inquit Eucleidēs. (is dangerous)

10. Ecce! Caesar _____ ; mox _____

   _____ . (has gotten up) (he will give the signal)

11. "Quibus aurīgīs _____ , Sexte?" rogat Marcus. (do you favor)

12. Ille aurīga, sī mētam _____ , vincet. (he avoids/he will have avoided)

13. Aurīga Marcī humī _____ . (was lying)

14. Spectātōrēs _____ _____ _____

_____ clāmābant. (the names of the charioteers and horses)

15. Cornēlia _____ clāmōrem numquam

_____ . (so great) (had heard)

Activity 27d
Fill in the blanks with Latin words to match the English cues:

1. "_____ liber _____ est,"
inquit Cornēlia. (This) (mine)

2. "Dā _____ _____ ," inquit
Flāvia. (it) (to me)

3. Marcus librōs _____ legere volēbat. (his own)

4. Nunc Marcus librōs _____ legere vult. (her)

5. "Estne hic _____ liber, Cornēlia?" (your)

6. "Liber _____ est." (his)

7. Aurīgae in curriculō _____ nocuērunt. (themselves)

8. "_____ nocuistī?" (Yourself)

9. "_____ nocēre nōlō." (Myself)

10. _____ nocēre nōlunt. (Themselves)

11. Cornēlius est senātor praeclārus; Sextus clientēs _____
domum intrantēs vīdit. (his)

12. "Hoc _____ , nōn amīcīs, fēcistis." (for yourselves)

13. "Pater _____ , puerī, in vīllam venīre iussit." (you)

14. "Necesse est _____ puerōs ad Circum dūcere." (for us)

15. "Nōlīte nocēre librīs _____ , puerī." (your)

16. "Librōs _____ cūrābimus, pater." (our)

17. "_____ nōn cōnfīdō, Geta." (you)

18. Multī Rōmānī servīs _____ nōn cōnfīdunt. (their own)

19. "Cōnfīdisne servīs _____ , Cornēlī?" (your)

20. "_____ cōnfīdō." (them)

Activity 27e

Change each verb from the tense in which it is given to each of the other tenses. Be sure to keep the same person and number as the given form:

Present	Imperfect	Future	Perfect	Pluperfect	Future Perfect
1.	erat				
2. iaceō					
3.		vetābis			
4.			potuit		
5.				ceciderant	
6.					volueritis
7.	aperiēbāmus				
8.		ībō	iī	ieram	ierō
9. arripit					
10.			tulērunt		

Activity 27f

Add the prefix to each simple verb below and give the meaning of the compound verb. Check the meanings in a Latin dictionary to be sure you have deduced them correctly:

Simple Verb	+	Prefix	=	Compound Verb (infinitive)	Meaning

1. movēre + prō- = _____ _____

2. surgere + re- = _____ _____

3. scrībere + prae- = _____ _____

4. portāre + ex- = _____ _____

5. venīre + con- = _____ _____

6. vocāre + in- = _____ _____

7. cēdere + dē- = _____ _____

8. pōnere + dis- = _____ _____

9. haerēre + ad- = _____ _____

Activity 27g

Give the meaning of each English word and the Latin compound verb from which it is derived. Note that Latin *ae* becomes English e:

English Word	*Meaning*	*Latin Compound Verb*
1. convention		
2. exports (noun)		
3. deceased (adj.)		
4. dispose		
5. promotion		
6. prescription		
7. adhere		
8. invocation		
9. resurgent		

VOCABULARY FOR REVIEW

Note: this list includes the demonstrative adjectives consolidated in Chapter 26, all 4th and 5th declension nouns that have appeared through Chapter 27, and all of the pronouns and possessive adjectives treated in Chapter 27.

NOUNS

1st Declension

Caligula, -ae, m., *Caligula (emperor, A.D. 37–41)*

causa, -ae, f., *reason*

glōria, -ae, f., *fame, glory*

mappa, -ae, f., *napkin*

mēta, -ae, f., *mark, goal, turning post*

poēta, -ae, m., *poet*

taberna, -ae, f., *shop*

terra, -ae, f., *earth, ground*

2nd Declension

amphitheātrum, -ī, n., *amphitheater*

ātrium, -ī, n., *atrium, main room*

bona, -ōrum, n. pl., *goods, possessions*

captīvus, -ī, m., *captive, prisoner*

colloquium, -ī, n., *conversation*

curriculum, -ī, n., *race track*

Forum, -ī, n., *the Forum (town center of Rome)*

gladius, -ī, m., *sword*

lūdus, -ī, m., *school*

lutum, -ī, n., *mud*

oculus, -ī, m., *eye*

patrōnus, -ī, m., *patron*

signum, -ī, n., *signal*

stilus, -ī, m., *pen*

tablīnum, -ī, n., *study*

vīnum, -ī, n., *wine*

3rd Declension

Caesar, Caesaris, m., *Caesar, emperor*

caput, capitis, n., *head*

cliēns, clientis, gen. pl., **clientium,** m., *client, dependent*

coniūnx, coniugis, m./f., *husband, wife*

custōs, custōdis, m., *guard*

factiō, factiōnis, f., *company (of charioteers)*

lapis, lapidis, m., *stone*

mulier, mulieris, f., *woman*

ōrātiō, ōrātiōnis, f., *oration, speech*

postis, postis, gen. pl., **postium,** m., *door-post*

praedō, praedōnis, m., *robber*

spectātor, spectātōris, m., *spectator*

victor, victōris, m., *conqueror, victor*

4th Declension

aestus, -ūs, m., *heat*

aquaeductus, -ūs, m., *aqueduct*

arcus, -ūs, m., *arch*

complexus, -ūs, m., *embrace*

domus, -ūs, f., *house*

manus, -ūs, f., *hand*

metus, -ūs, m., *fear*

reditus, -ūs, m., *return*

rīsus, -ūs, m., *smile, laugh*

senātus, -ūs, m., *Senate*

sonitus, -ūs, m., *sound*

strepitus, -ūs, m., *noise, clattering*

tumultus, -ūs, m., *uproar, commotion*

5th Declension

diēs, diēī, m., *day*

rēs, reī, f., *thing, matter, situation*

ADJECTIVES

1st and 2nd Declension

albātus, -a, -um, *white*

antīquus, -a, -um, *ancient*

aureus, -a, -um, *golden*

excitātus, -a, -um, *wakened, aroused*

fēriātus, -a, -um, *celebrating a holiday*

meus, -a, -um, *my, my own, mine*

noster, nostra, nostrum, *our, our own, ours*

oppressus, -a, -um, *crushed*

parvulus, -a, -um, *small, little*

prasinus, -a, -um, *green*

quadrātus, -a, -um, *squared*

quīntus, -a, -um, *fifth*

russātus, -a, -um, *red*

suus, -a, -um, *his own, her own, its own, their own*

tertius, -a, -um, *third*

tuus, -a, -um, *your, your own, yours (sing.)*

venetus, -a, -um, *blue*

verbōsus, -a, -um, *talkative*

vester, vestra, vestrum, *your, your own, yours (pl.)*

3rd Declension

circēnsis, -is, -e, *in the circus*

immortālis, -is, -e, *immortal*

VERBS

1st Conjugation

dēsīderō, -āre, -āvī, -ātus, *to long for, miss*

servō, -āre, -āvī, -ātus, *to save*

vetō, vetāre, vetuī, vetitus, *to forbid*

2nd Conjugation

dēbeō, -ēre, -uī, -itūrus + infin., *ought*

faveō, favēre, fāvī, fautūrus + dat., *to give favor (to), favor, support*

iaceō, -ēre, -uī, -itūrus, *to lie, be lying down*

noceō, -ēre, -uī, -itūrus + dat., *to do harm (to), harm*

teneō, tenēre, tenuī, tentus, *to hold*

3rd Conjugation

accidit, accidere, accidit, *it happens*

claudō, claudere, clausī, clausus, *to shut*

cōnfīdō, cōnfīdere + dat., *to give trust (to), trust*

dēvertō, dēvertere, dēvertī, dēversus, *to turn aside*

stertō, stertere, stertuī, *to snore*

stringō, stringere, strīnxī, strictus,
to draw

trahō, trahere, trāxī, tractus, *to drag, pull*

vincō, vincere, vīcī, victus, *to conquer, win*

3rd Conjugation -iō

arripiō, arripere, arripuī, arreptus, *to grab hold of, snatch, seize*

fugiō, fugere, fūgī, fugitūrus, *to flee*

cōnficiō, cōnficere, cōnfēcī, cōnfectus, *to finish*

4th Conjugation

aperiō, aperīre, aperuī, apertus, *to open*

perveniō, pervenīre, pervēnī, perventūrus + ad + acc., *to arrive (at), reach*

sciō, scīre, scīvī, scītus, *to know*

Irregular

absum, abesse, āfuī, āfutūrus, *to be away, be absent, be distant*

adsum, adesse, adfuī, adfutūrus, *to be present*

PRONOUNS

aliquid, *something*

ego, *I*

eī, eae, ea, *they*

eius, *of him, of her, his, hers, its*

eōrum, *of them, their*

is, ea, id, *he, she, it*

nōs, *we*

quās, f. pl., acc., *which*

quod, n. sing., nom. or acc., *which*

suī, sibi, sē, sē, *himself, herself, oneself, itself, themselves*

tū, *you* (sing.)

vōs, *you* (pl.)

PREPOSITIONS

apud + acc., *with, in front of, before*

propter + acc., *on account of, because of*

sine + abl., *without*

ADVERBS

abhinc, *ago, previously*

aliter, *otherwise*

nōnnumquam, *sometimes*

postrīdiē, *on the following day*

ut, *as*

CONJUNCTIONS

aut . . . aut . . . , *either . . . or . . .*

nisi, *unless, if . . . not, except*

INTERROGATIVE WORD

Quōcum . . . ? *With whom . . . ?* (sing.)

MISCELLANEOUS

domī, *at home*

Eho! *Hey!*

eō diē, *on that day*

gladium stringere, *to draw a sword*

Grātiās tibi agō! *I thank you! Thank you!*

hic, haec, hoc, *this*
huius, *of this*

humī, *on the ground*

ille, illa, illud, *that*

lūdī circēnsēs, *chariot-racing*

Mōns Vesuvius, *Mount Vesuvius (a volcano in southern Italy)*

ōrātiōnem habēre, *to deliver a speech*

sequēns, sequentis, *following*

sī vīs, *if you wish, please*

Activity VIa
Translate into Latin:

1. "All those famous citizens," said Apollodorus, "wanted to dine and spend the night at this inn."

_____

_____

2. When the slaves with much labor bring/will have brought a better bed into the bedroom, Cornelia and Aurelia will go to sleep.

_____

_____

3. Marcus and Sextus may stay awake for many hours after dinner.

_____

4. Aulus appeared to his friend in a dream and shouted to him, "Come, Septimus, help me! The innkeeper intends to kill me tonight."

_____

_____

5. Near the city the boys will catch sight of huge tombs of many famous citizens.

_____

6. While Cornelius was taking Aurelia and Cornelia home, Titus was showing the boys many wonderful things in the city.

_____

_____

7. Cornelius, who had already arrived at the Arch of Tiberius, met Titus and the boys there.

_____

_____

8. When the boys have had/will have had enough time to examine all the buildings in the Forum, it will be getting dark.

_____

_____

9. One of those robbers had already seized this boy and was dragging him into that house.

_____

_____

10. When the boys see/will have seen the charioteers, they will leave the Circus Maximus and return home.

_____

_____

Activity VIb

Read the following passage and write answers in Latin to the questions below:

Vir quīdam praeclārus, nōmine Ulixēs, ab urbe Troiā redībat et uxōrem suam
Pēnelopam vidēre volēbat. Diū tamen eī nōn licēbat domum redīre, nam Neptūnus, deus
maris, īrātus cōnstituerat eum pūnīre quod Ulixēs, fīliō Neptūnī nocuerat. Hūc illūc igitur
per multa maria errābat Ulixēs, multās īnsulās vīsitābat, multa et mīra animālia vidēbat.
Identidem deus eum in mare praecipitābat, identidem Ulixēs incolumis effugiēbat.   5

Ubi ad īnsulam quandam vēnit, servāvit eum dea, nōmine Calypsō, quae ibi habitābat.
Cibum et vestēs dedit; virum diū cūrābat; mox eum amābat et uxor eius esse volēbat. Sed
Ulixēs dē uxōre suā cōgitābat. Sōlus saepe lacrimābat neque volēbat in illā īnsulā manēre.
Dea, ubi eum lacrimantem cōnspexit, "Cūr dolēs?" inquit. Ulixēs, "Dē Pēnelopā
cōgitābam," respondit. "Quamquam mē bene cūrās et multa mihi dās, tamen domum redīre   10
volō."

Tandem dea servōs iussit nāvem, cibum, vestēs parāre, nam nōluit eum retinēre invītum.

1. Quem Ulixēs vidēre volēbat?

_____

2. Cūr diū eī nōn licēbat domum redīre?

_____

3. Quō Ulixēs errābat?

_____

4. Quid vidēbat?

_____

5. Quis eum in mare praecipitābat?

_____

6. Quis eum servāvit?

_____

7. Quid ea volēbat?

_____

8. Dē quā Ulixēs cōgitābat?

_____

9. Quid saepe faciēbat?

_____

10. Quid volēbat?

_____

11. Quid tandem dea fēcit?

_____

12. Cūr id fēcit?

_____

Ulixēs, Ulixis, m.,
  Ulysses, Odysseus

deus, -ī, m., *god*

mare, maris, n., *sea*

īnsula, -ae, f., *island*

vestis, vestis, gen. pl.,
  vestium, f., *garment*

nāvis, nāvis, gen. pl.,
  nāvium, f., *ship*

Activity VIc

Find and circle the Latin words for the English words listed to the right. Words may go in a horizontal, vertical, or diagonal direction, but they are never backward.

```
e a v n x p z n d b c a p u t
b s d u a a o z u e i e f d t
p g t n h b e s g n i t l f a
r k a o l h i m t h c o a p n
o t m a l i q u i d a k p q d
p a b h i n r l n o r m i s u
i m t o a c b t a m e i d o m
f e v t p o s t r i d i e x p
y o t a s r z f o r t a s i f
a v r i l u o l a p i t e s b
e c y t x i d p z e t a m e n
f s c a a b q a e h g n e q e
e h t q f s e u k d l d o m q
h m r u l n s k i h o e g p u
o q y e x r v e s b t m s u e
```

1. on the following day
2. at home
3. ago, previously
4. something
5. stones
6. perhaps
7. all right!
8. and so
9. hey!
10. now
11. head
12. and . . . not
13. near
14. however, nevertheless
15. at last

Activity VId

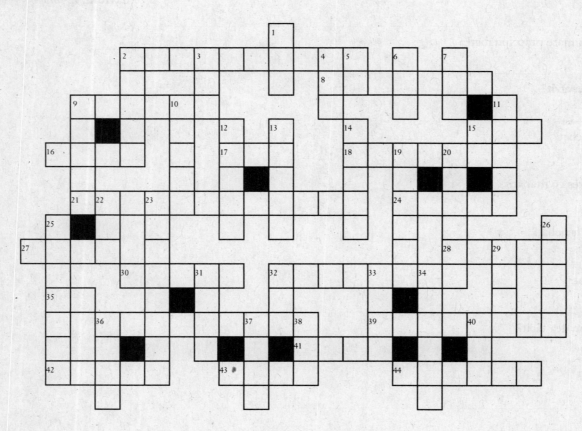

ACROSS

2. you (pl.) are allowed
8. **vidēs:** change to future perf.
9. **vetuerat:** change to perf.
15. **haec:** change to sing.
16. for
17. **rērum:** change to sing.
18. **advenītis:** change to sing.
21. with a great uproar
24. **colēbam:** change to perf.
27. without
28. opposite of **aliquid**
30. **rē:** change to pl.
32. **dormīverant:** change to fut.
35. as
36. **praedō:** change to pl.
39. **lectīcam:** change to pl.
41. **urbibus:** change to sing.
42. **cecidit:** change to pres.
43. **illīs:** change to abl. sing.
44. **ferunt:** change to fut.

DOWN

1. **ego:** change to pl.
2. **lutō:** change to nom. sing.
3. **erit:** change to pres.
4. **ībam:** change to perf. with stem **īv-**
5. if
6. **rēs:** change to acc. sing.
7. **hī:** change to sing.
9. **vīnī:** change to nom. sing.
10. **iacēmus:** change to sing.
11. **pōnam:** change to perf.
12. **arcibus:** change to dat. sing.
13. **rīsus:** change to acc. sing.
14. **manuum:** change to sing.
15. **hae:** change to masc.
19. to call
20. **nōn vult:** change to pl.
22. **agite:** change to sing.
23. **nocent:** change to imperf.
25. as soon as
26. **illō:** change to pl.
29. **hōs:** change to sing.
31. where . . . from?
32. **diēbus:** change to sing.
33. **ille:** change to pl.
34. **noctēs:** change to sing.
36. **pēs:** change to abl. sing.
37. **nōluī:** change to pres.
38. **suus, -a, -um:** make agree with **patre**
40. to go

PART 1
IN THE FORUM

Activity 1a
Translate:

Heri, quod occupātī erant et Cornēlius et Titus, Eucleidēs ipse puerōs et Cornēliam in 1
urbem dūcere in animō habēbat. "Eugepae!" clāmāvit Sextus. "Ostendēsne nōbīs Forum 2
atque aedificia?" 3

"Ita vērō," respondit Eucleidēs, "imprīmīs illa aedificia quae—" 4

Eucleidēs rem explicāre nōn poterat quod puerī iam ē domō exierant et per viās urbis 5
praecurrēbant. Necesse erat Eucleidī et Cornēliae festīnāre. Mox ad Forum advēnērunt 6
ubi Eucleidēs et Cornēlia puerōs prope arcum Tiberiī invēnērunt. "Hic est arcus," inquit 7
Eucleidēs, "ubi pater vester heri nōbīs occurrit. Imperātor Tiberius hunc arcum—" 8

"Ecce," interpellāvit Sextus. "Quālis statua est illa?" 9

Marcus Sextō magnō rīsū respondit, "Nōn est statua, stulte! Ille est umbilīcus orbis 10
terrārum." 11

"Ita vērō," inquit Cornēlia. "Est mīliārium aureum, quod Caesar Augustus posuit." 12

Sextus tamen nōn audiēbat, sed subitō, "Age, Marce!" inquit et per Viam Sacram 13
currēbat. Ubi Eucleidēs tandem puerōs cōnsecūtus est, Sextus eum rogāvit, "Quid est 14
illud aedificium?" 15

"Illa est Basilica Iūlia," respondit Eucleidēs. 16

"Aedificāvitne illam basilicam Iūlius Caesar?" rogāvit Sextus. 17

"Ita vērō," respondit Eucleidēs. "Dīvus Iūlius hanc basilicam aedificāvit atque tōtum—" 18
Sextus tamen iterum praecurrerat. 19

Multās hōrās puerī et puella Eucleidem per urbem dūcēbant. Multa dē aedificiīs 20
rogābant. Decimā hōrā tandem domuī appropinquābant. Nōndum tamen erat tempus 21
cēnāre; līberī igitur ad hortum festīnāvērunt, Eucleidēs ad cubiculum. 22

Glossary (margin):

2 **ostendō, ostendere, ostendī, ostentus,** *to show*

4 **imprīmīs,** adv., *especially*

10 **umbilīcus orbis terrārum,** *center of the universe; lit., navel of the circle of the lands*

orbis, orbis, gen. pl., **orbium,** m., *circle, ring*

11 **terra, -ae,** f., *earth, land*

12 **mīliārium -ī,** n., *milestone*

13 **sacer, sacra, sacrum,** *sacred*

14 **cōnsecūtus est,** *(he) overtook*

16 **Basilica Iūlia, -ae,** f., *Basilica Julia (one of Rome's law courts)*

18 **dīvus -a,-um,** *divine*

21 **decimus, -a, -um,** *tenth*

_____

_____

_____

_____

_____

_____

_____

_____

Activity 1b

Match each word at the left (taken from the designated line in the reading passage above) first with its case and then with its use within the phrase or sentence in which it occurs:

A. Nominative
B. Genitive
C. Dative
D. Accusative
E. Ablative
F. Vocative

a. subject
b. direct object
c. with intransitive verb
d. with preposition
e. time
f. possession
g. direct address
h. manner

1. puerōs (1) _____ _____

2. aedificia (3) _____ _____

3. rem (5) _____ _____

4. puerī (5) _____ _____

5. domō (5) _____ _____

6. urbis (5) _____ _____

7. arcum (7) _____ _____

8. hic (7) _____ _____

9. Sextō (10) _____ _____

10. rīsū (10) _____ _____

11. orbis (10) _____ _____

12. terrārum (11) _____ _____

13. Marce (13) _____ _____

14. basilicam (17) _____ _____

15. urbem (20) _____ _____

16. aedificiīs (20) _____ _____

17. hōrā (21) _____ _____

Activity 1c

Change every noun in Exercise 1b above that is not a proper noun to its plural form if it is singular and to its singular form if it is plural. Be sure to keep the same case:

1. puerōs _____

2. aedificia _____

3. rem _____

4. puerī _____

5. domō _____

6. urbis _____

7. arcum _____

8. amīcō _____

9. rīsū _____

10. orbis _____

11. terrārum _____

12. basilicam _____

13. urbem _____

14. aedificiīs _____

15. hōrā _____

Activity 1d

Modify the nouns listed in Exercise 1b (excepting, again, the proper nouns) with the correct forms of the adjectives *parvulus, -a, -um* and *ingēns, ingentis*:

1. puerōs _____ _____
2. aedificia _____ _____
3. rem _____ _____
4. puerī _____ _____
5. domō _____ _____
6. urbis _____ _____
7. arcum _____ _____
8. amīcō _____ _____
9. rīsū _____ _____
10. orbis _____ _____
11. terrārum _____ _____
12. basilicam _____ _____
13. urbem _____ _____
14. aedificiīs _____ _____
15. hōrā _____ _____

Activity 1e

Modify the nouns you used in Exercise 1d above with the correct forms of the demonstrative adjectives *hic, haec, hoc* and *ille, illa, illud*:

1. puerōs _____ _____
2. aedificia _____ _____
3. rem _____ _____
4. puerī _____ _____
5. domō _____ _____
6. urbis _____ _____
7. arcum _____ _____
8. amīcō _____ _____
9. rīsū _____ _____
10. orbis _____ _____
11. terrārum _____ _____
12. basilicam _____ _____
13. urbem _____ _____
14. aedificiīs _____ _____
15. hōrā _____ _____

Activity 1f

Write out all forms of the following seven nouns from the story:

1. basilicam (17)   *Singular*   *Plural*

Nom.   _____   _____

Gen.   _____   _____

Dat.   _____   _____

Acc.   _____   _____

Abl.   _____   _____

Voc.   _____   _____

2. umbilīcus (10)   *Singular*   *Plural*

Nom.   _____   _____

Gen.   _____   _____

Dat.   _____   _____

Acc.   _____   _____

Abl.   _____   _____

Voc.   _____   _____

3. aedificium (15)   *Singular*   *Plural*

Nom.   _____   _____

Gen.   _____   _____

Dat.   _____   _____

Acc.   _____   _____

Abl.   _____   _____

Voc.   _____   _____

4. pater (8)   *Singular*   *Plural*

Nom.   _____   _____

Gen.   _____   _____

Dat.   _____   _____

Acc.   _____   _____

Abl.   _____   _____

Voc.   _____   _____   **(continued)**

5. tempus (21)   *Singular*   *Plural*

Nom. _____   _____

Gen. _____   _____

Dat. _____   _____

Acc. _____   _____

Abl. _____   _____

Voc. _____   _____

6. arcus (7)   *Singular*   *Plural*

Nom. _____   _____

Gen. _____   _____

Dat. _____   _____

Acc. _____   _____

Abl. _____   _____

Voc. _____   _____

7. rem (5)   *Singular*   *Plural*

Nom. _____   _____

Gen. _____   _____

Dat. _____   _____

Acc. _____   _____

Abl. _____   _____

Voc. _____   _____

Activity 1g

Translate the following phrases into English. Then rewrite the phrases by making all singular nouns plural and all plural nouns singular. Make sure you keep the nouns in the same case:

1. ē manibus _____

_____

2. sub lapide _____

_____

3. per viās _____

_____

4. sine custōde _____

_____

5. dē somniō mīlitis _____

_____

6. prope mētam _____

_____

7. intrā aedificia _____

_____

8. cum mulieribus _____

_____

9. ā portā _____

_____

10. in lectīcās _____

_____

11. ad amphitheātrum _____

_____

12. post cēnam _____

_____

Activity1h
Translate the following phrases into Latin without using prepositions:

1. at dawn _____

2. for us _____

3. at home _____

4. to the poets _____

5. with a great uproar _____

6. by a sign _____

7. for the soldier _____

8. to me _____

9. homeward _____

10. from the heat _____

11. for Cornelius _____

12. to Aurelia _____

PART 2
TO THE RACES AGAIN

Activity 2a
Read aloud and translate:

13 **bene,** *well*

nōverat, *(he) knew*

14 **bellus, -a, -um,** *beautiful*

melius, *better*

15 **cursus, -ūs,** m., *race, racing*

certāmen, certāminis, n., *contest*

aliās, adv., *sometimes*

16 **saepissimē,** adv., *most often*

ā tergō, *from behind*

17 **Heus!** *Hey!*

Iam quīnta hōra erat. Necesse erat Titō Sextum et Marcum et Cornēliam ad Circum 1
Maximum dūcere quod Cornēlius iterum ad Cūriam ierat et Eucleidēs aberat. Līberī cum 2
patruō iam Montem Palātīnum circumierant et Circō appropinquābant. 3

"Eugepae," identidem clāmābat Sextus, quī aurīgās spectāre valdē volēbat. "Hodiē meī 4
russātī certē vincent." 5

"Ego," inquit Titus, "prasinīs semper faveō." 6

"Ego quoque prasinīs hodiē faveō," respondit Marcus quod patruum valdē amābat. 7

Cornēlia tamen, "Ego adhūc venetīs faveō." 8

Ubi Circum intrāvērunt, Marcus Titum rogāvit, "Licetne nōbīs, patrue, prope 9
curriculum sedēre?" 10

"Estō," inquit Titus, quī prope curriculum cum amīcīs suīs sedēre solēbat. "Nisi prope 11
curriculum consēderimus, prīncipem nōn cōnspiciēmus." 12

"Neque aurīgās," mussāvit Sextus, quī Titum bene nōverat. 13

"Neque bellās puellās," respondit Marcus, quī Titum melius nōverat. 14

Marcus et Sextus et Cornēlia multa cursūs certāmina vidēre poterant. Aliās prasinī, aliās 15
russātī vincēbant. Saepissimē tamen vincēbant venetī. Subitō homō quīdam Marcum ā tergō 16
ferīvit. "Heus tū!" exclāmāvit Marcus, "Cavē! Nōlī mē ferīre! Sī tū fīliō senātōris nocueris, 17
pater meus tē certē—" 18

"Tacē, Marce," interpellāvit Titus. "Nōlī illum hominem vexāre! Praetereā, tempus est 19
nōbīs domum redīre. Pater vester nōs exspectābit." 20

Titus igitur līberōs invītōs ē Circō domum per viās urbis dūxit. 21

Activity 2b

Identify the tense, person, and number of the following verbs (taken from the designated line of the reading passage). Then write the principal parts of each verb:

1. aberat (2) _____ _____ _____

   _____

2. circumierant (3) _____ _____ _____

   _____

3. volēbat (4) _____ _____ _____

   _____

4. vincent (5) _____ _____ _____

   _____

5. faveō (6) _____ _____ _____

   _____

6. intrāvērunt (9) _____ _____ _____

   _____

7. cōnspiciēmus (12) _____ _____ _____

   _____

8. mussāvit (13) _____ _____ _____

   _____

9. poterant (15) _____ _____ _____

   _____

10. ferīvit (17) _____ _____ _____

    _____

11. nocueris (17) _____ _____ _____

    _____

Activity 2c

Using the same verbs listed in Exercise 2b, write out all six tenses of the verb, keeping the same person and number:

	Present	Imperfect	Future	Perfect	Pluperfect	Future Perfect
1.						
2.						
3.						
4.						
5.						
6.						
7.						
8.						
9.						
10.						
11.						

Activity 2d

Complete the following sentences by filling in each blank with a present infinitive. Use different verbs in each sentence. Make sure your sentences make sense. Then translate the sentences into English:

1. Sextus omnia aedificia in urbis _____ volēbat.

   _____

2. Cornēlia hodiē ad Circum Maximum _____ nōn vult.

   _____

3. Puerī ad mediam noctem _____ in animō habēbant.

   _____

4. Nōs sine custōde in urbem _____ timēbāmus.

   _____

5. Ego vōs in cubiculīs _____ iussī.

   _____

6. Potesne fābulam mīlitis mihi _____?

   _____

7. Licet nōbīs hīc _____.

   _____

Activity 2e

Give the imperatives of the following verbs, singular and plural, positive and negative:

	Sing.	Pl.	Sing.	Pl.
1. cōgitāre				
2. pūnīre				
3. dūcere				
4. ferre				
5. venīre				
6. pōnere				

Activity 2f

Give the appropriate personal pronoun in the nominative case to match the ending of each verb:

1. cōgitās _____

2. docēbimus _____

3. circumībāmus _____

4. puniētis _____

5. scīvistis _____

6. pervēneris _____

7. sūmpserō _____

8. nārrābam _____

9. vetō _____

10. nocuerātis _____

11. coniēcistī _____

12. iēcerāmus _____

Activity 2g

Match each verb form at the left with its proper translation:

1. vīdit _____
2. ferēbās _____
3. vīderat _____
4. pūnīvimus _____
5. tulistī _____
6. pūnīverāmus _____
7. vidēbat _____
8. fers _____
9. vīderit _____
10. pūnīverimus _____
11. ferēs _____
12. tulerās _____
13. pūniēmus _____
14. tuleris _____
15. pūnīmus _____
16. videt _____
17. vidēbit _____
18. pūniēbāmus _____

a. we have punished
b. he had seen
c. we are punishing
d. you will bring
e. you carry
f. we had punished
g. he sees
h. you brought
i. she will see
j. we will punish
k. we began to punish
l. she will have seen
m. you had brought
n. we will have punished
o. he saw
p. she used to see
q. you will have brought
r. you were carrying

Activity 2h

Give a compound verb formed from each of the following verbs. Give all principal parts for each compound:

1. dūcō _____
2. faciō _____
3. eō _____
4. sum _____
5. ferō _____
6. cēdō _____
7. iaciō _____
8. veniō _____